Alto Saxophone

INSTRUMENTAL PLAY-ALONG

JAZZ CLASSICS

Contents

TITLE	PAGE	
Bernie's Tune	2	
Desafinado	4	
Fever	6	
Fly Me To The Moon (In Other Words)	8	4
God Bless' The Child	10	5
A Night In Tunisia	12	6
One Note Samba (Samba De Uma Nota So)	14	7
Satin Doll	16	8
Stompin' At The Savoy	18	9
Take The "A" Train	20	10
Woodchopper's Ball	19	11
Yardbird Suite	22	12
B♭ Tuning Notes		13
A Tuning Notes		14

HOW TO USE THE CD ACCOMPANIMENT:
A melody cue appears on the right channel only. If your CD player has a balance adjustment, you can adjust the volume of the melody by turning down the right channel.

This publication is not authorised for sale in the United States of America and/or Canada

Exclusive Distributors:
Music Sales Limited
14-15 Berners Street, London W1T 3LJ, UK.

Order No. HLE90003067
ISBN: 978-1-84609-591-7

Printed in the USA

Your Guarantee of Quality
As publishers, we strive to produce every book to the highest commercial standards. The book has been carefully designed to minimise awkward page turns and to make playing from it a real pleasure. Throughout, the printing and binding have been planned to ensure a sturdy, attractive publication which should give years of enjoyment. If your copy fails to meet our high standards, please inform us and we will gladly replace it.

www.musicsales.com

HLE
HAL LEONARD EUROPE
DISTRIBUTED BY MUSIC SALES

1 BERNIE'S TUNE

Music by BERNIE MILLER

F♯7
B mi
55
C♯7
F♯7
59
B mi
End Solo
Piano Solo
7
mf
63
Piano Solo
7
mf
74
8
sfp
85
mf
97
102
107
8
mf
111
D.S. al Coda
(with repeat)
123
Coda
f
129

2 DESAFINADO

ALTO SAX

Original Text by NEWTON MENDONCA
Music by ANTONIO CARLOS JOBIM

To Coda
2
Solo-ad lib. or as written
D9(♯11)
mp
Dmi7
G7
Emi7(♭5)
mp
A7(♭9)
Dmi
Fmi6
Cma7
End Solo
D.S. al Coda
Coda
rall.

3 FEVER

ALTO SAX

Words and Music by
JOHN DAVENPORT and EDDIE COOLEY

G♯mi7
F♯mi7
G♯mi7
F♯mi7
G♯mi7
F♯mi7
G♯mi7
F♯mi7
G♯mi7
F♯mi7
G♯mi7
C♯7
F♯mi7
G♯mi7
F♯mi7
G♯mi7
F♯mi7
G♯mi7
F♯mi7
G♯mi7
F♯mi7
G♯mi7
F♯mi7
G♯mi7
C♯7
F♯mi
End Solo
Straight 8ths
mf
D.S. al Coda
Coda
f
mp

4 FLY ME TO THE MOON
(In Other Words)

ALTO SAX

Words and Music by
BART HOWARD

Gmi7 C7 Fma7 Dmi7
Gmi7 C7 Fma7 Emi7(♭5) A7
Dmi7 Gmi7 C7 Fma7 B♭ma7
Emi7(♭5) A7 Dmi7 Gmi7 C7
Ami7(♭5) D7 Gmi7 C7
F Emi7(♭5) A7
End Solo
Piano Solo
D.S. al Coda
(with repeat)
7
Coda

5 GOD BLESS' THE CHILD

featured in the Motion Picture LADY SINGS THE BLUES

ALTO SAX

Words and Music by
ARTHUR HERZOG JR. and BILLIE HOLIDAY

Medium slow tempo (♩= 78) (♫ = ♩♪ triplet)

25
mf
29
mp
33
36
39
Organ Solo
4
43
47
mf
50
54

6 A NIGHT IN TUNISIA

ALTO SAX

Music by JOHN "DIZZY" GILLESPIE
and FRANK PAPARELLI

To Coda
Solo-ad lib. or as written
B♭9
Ami6
B♭9
Ami6
B♭9
Ami6
Bmi7(♭5)
E7
Ami6
B♭9
Ami6
B♭9
Ami6
B♭9
Ami6
Bmi7(♭5)
E7(♭9)
Ami
Emi7(♭5)
A7
Dmi
A7
Dmi
Fmi6
G7
Cma7
Bmi7(♭5)
E7(♯9)
B♭9
Ami6
B♭9
Ami6
D.S. al Coda
(with repeat)
B♭9
Ami6
Bmi7(♭5)
E7(♯9)
Ami
End Solo
Coda
f

7 ONE NOTE SAMBA

(Samba De Uma Nota So)

ALTO SAX

Original Lyrics by NEWTON MENDONCA
English Lyrics by ANTONIO CARLOS JOBIM
Music by ANTONIO CARLOS JOBIM

poco cresc.
mf
To Coda
mp
Piano Solo
8
Solo-ad lib. or as written
G♯mi7
G9(♯11)
F♯mi7
F9(♯11)
Bmi7
B♭9(♯11)
Ami7
D7
G6
F♯7
F7
E
D.S. al Coda
End Solo
Coda

8 SATIN DOLL

from SOPHISTICATED LADIES

ALTO SAX

By DUKE ELLINGTON

Solo-ad lib. or as written
Bmi7 E7 Bmi7 E7 C♯mi7 F♯7
30
C♯mi7 F♯7 F♯mi7 B7 Fmi7 B♭7
33
A C♯mi7 F♯7 Bmi7 E7
36
Bmi7 E7 C♯mi7 F♯7 C♯mi7 F♯7
39
F♯mi7 B7 Fmi7 B♭7 A
42
Piano Solo
7
Bmi7 E7 Bmi7 E7
46
C♯mi7 F♯7 C♯mi F♯7 F♯mi7 B7
56
Fmi7 B♭7 Ama7
D.S. al Coda
End Solo
59
Coda
mf
62

9 STOMPIN' AT THE SAVOY

ALTO SAX

By BENNY GOODMAN,
EDGAR SAMPSON and CHICK WEBB

Relaxed Swing (♩= 120)

11 WOODCHOPPER'S BALL

By JOE BISHOP
and WOODY HERMAN

ALTO SAX

Medium Fast Swing (♩= 168)

10 TAKE THE "A" TRAIN

ALTO SAX

Words and Music by
BILLY STRAYHORN

Piano Solo
Solo-ad lib. or as written
B7
Bmi
E7
Bb7
A
B7
Piano Solo
Solo-ad lib. or as written
A
B7
Bmi7
E7
A
A#o
Bmi7
E7
A
B7
Bmi7
E7
A
Emi7
A7
D
B7
Bmi7
E7
A
B7
D.S. al Coda (with repeat)
Bmi7
E7
A
Bmi7
E7
Coda

Listen!
Think!
Feel!
Pencil.....

12 YARDBIRD SUITE

ALTO SAX

By CHARLIE PARKER

C7 B7 E7 Emi7 D#7(b5) Dma7 Gmi C7
Dma7 C7 B7 E7 Emi7 A7 D
short
tongued
Emi7 A7
End Solo
Piano Solo
Solo-ad lib. or as written
End Piano Solo
Dma7 Gmi C7
mf
Dma7 C7 B7 E7 Emi7 A7
F#mi7 B7 Emi7 D#7(b5) Dma7 Gmi C7
Dma7 C7 B7 E7 Emi7 A7
D C#7
End Solo
Piano Solo
Solo
Dma7
mf
Gmi C7 Dma7 C7 B7 E7
D.S. al Coda (with repeat)
Emi7 A7 D Emi7 A7
End Solo
Coda